THEATRE 503

BU21

BY STUART SLADE

BU21 was first performed at Theatre503, London, in association with Kuleshov, on 15 March 2016

BU21
BY STUART SLADE

CAST

Alex	Alex Forsyth
Ana	Roxana Lupu
Clive	Clive Keene
Floss	Florence Roberts
Graham	Graham O'Mara
Thalissa	Thalissa Teixeira

CREATIVE TEAM

Director	Dan Pick
Producer	Holly Hooper
Assistant Director	Kane Desborough
Production Design	Alex Green
Sound Design	Owen Crouch
Lighting Design	Christopher Nairne
Assistant Stage Manager	Lottie Mclarin
Fight Coordinator	Lucy Slade
Marketing Design	Lucy Newman, Neni Almeida
Casting	Danny Scollard, Kate Evans
Head of Literary	Sarah Page
PR	Chloe Nelkin Consulting
Voice Coaches	Elitza Goudemand, Iva Manolova, Mellie Naydenova-Slade

kuleshov

BU21 is Production #6 from Kuleshov.

Kuleshov is a theatre company committed to developing innovative and powerful new writing. It is led by Dan Pick and Stuart Slade, with Holly Hooper as Producer and Sarah Page as Head of Literary.

www.kuleshovtheatre.com

Corporate Partners

Kuleshov is very lucky to have two very lovely corporate sponsors, without which this play would simply not have been possible. Thank you, guys!

THEATRE 503

Theatre503 is the award-winning home of groundbreaking plays.

Led by Artistic Director Paul Robinson, Theatre503 is a flagship fringe venue committed to producing new work that is topical, thrilling and theatrical. We are the smallest theatre to win an Olivier award and we offer more opportunities to new writers than any other theatre in the UK.

THEATRE503 TEAM

Artistic Director	Paul Robinson
Executive Director	Jeremy Woodhouse
Producer and Head of Marketing	Jessica Campbell
Associate Artistic Director	Lisa Cagnacci
Literary Manager	Steve Harper
Literary Coordinators	Lauretta Barrow, Tom Latter
Office Manager	Anna De Freitas
Resident Assistant Producers	Kate Powell, Jack Paterson, Robyn Bennett
Theatre503 Intern	Sam Read
Volunteer Coordinators	Serafina Cusack, Simon Mander
Associate Directors	Anna Jordan, Jonathan O'Boyle
Senior Readers	Karis Halsall, Kate Brower, Clare O'Hara, Jimmy Osborne, Imogen Sarre

THEATRE503 BOARD

Royce Bell, Peter Benson, Chris Campbell, Kay Ellen Consolver, Ben Hall, Dennis Kelly, Eleanor Lloyd, Marcus Markou, Geraldine Sharpe-Newton, Jack Tilbury, Erica Whyman (Chair), Roy Williams.

And we couldn't do what we do without our volunteers:

Andrei Vornicu, Annabel Pemberton, Bethany Doherty, Charlotte Mulliner, Chidi Chukwu, Damian Robertson, Danielle Wilson, Fabienne Gould, George Linfield, James Hansen, Joanna Lallay, Kelly Agredo, Ken Hawes, Larner Taylor, Mandy Nicholls, Mark Doherty, Mike Murgaz, Nicole Marie, Rahim Dhanji, Rosie Akerman, Tess Hardy.

Theatre503 is supported by:

Philip and Chris Carne, Cas Donald, Gregory Dunlop, Angela Hyde-Courtney and the Audience Club, Stephanie Knauf, Sumintra Latchman, Katherine Malcom, Georgia Oetker, Francesca Ortona, Geraldine Sharpe-Newton.

Support Theatre503

Help us take risks on new writers and produce the plays other theatres can't, or won't. Together we can discover the writers of tomorrow and make some of the most exciting theatre in the country. With memberships ranging from £23 to £1003 there is a chance to get involved no matter what your budget, to help us remain 'arguably the most important theatre in Britain today' (*Guardian*).

Benefits range from priority notice of our work and news, access to sold out shows, ticket deals, and opportunities to attend parties and peek into rehearsals. Visit theatre503.com or call 020 7978 7040 for more details.

Theatre503, 503 Battersea Park Rd, London SW11 3BW
020 7978 7040 | www.theatre503.com
@Theatre503 | Facebook.com/theatre503

BU21

Stuart Slade

This play is dedicated, with love,
to Mellie Naydenova-Slade,
lifelong plane-crash aficionado and inspiration for this story.

4

Characters

ALEX, *twenty-four*
ANA, *twenty-five*
CLIVE, *nineteen*
FLOSS, *twenty-one*
GRAHAM, *twenty-nine*
THALISSA, *twenty-two*

*In performance, actors' real names should replace these
character names wherever possible.*

Note

*Where Ana mentions the year on page 7, this should be updated
as appropriate. It should correspond to the July immediately
after the date of performance.*

*This text went to press before the end of rehearsals and so may
differ slightly from the play as performed.*

Prologue

THALISSA *comes on to the stage alone.*

THALISSA. So – I – okay –

So you know how on the news these days there's just this endless stream of *horrendous* shit going down, like every single night? Suicide bombs, mass shootings, genocides, drone strikes, school massacres – it's like the end of the world or something.

And it feels sort of *voyeuristic* to watch it, but sort of *disrespectful* to switch it off.

And you're sitting there and part of you feels really heartbroken for the people caught up in that day's headline – and you're kind of like – 'Could I even *cope* if that stuff happened to me? Or would I just – (*Gestures 'fall to pieces'.*)

But then you're all like, 'Nah, that's totally never going to happen to me – right? That's a somebody-else thing, not a me thing.'

Because you can't literally conceive of it happening to you.

And then it does. It does happen to you.

And nothing prepares you for how fucking fierce it is.

Scene One

Immediately after the previous scene – perhaps a change of lights/music.

Long pause.

THALISSA. So I found out my mum was dead on Twitter. Which wasn't, you know, great.

Yeah.

It was about ten-thirty on a Friday morning and I was just printing off some stuff for a client workshop at eleven, and the printer was being just – *you fucking* – you know?

And then – out of absolutely nowhere – there was just this massive, massive bang –

It was even like a *sound* – it was just this, I don't even know the word – this pure *violence*.

And I guess I must have been knocked down by the blast – because I realised I was on the floor, so I got up – and I was deaf, like my ears were underwater –

And I looked up, and all the windows of the office were broken, and I was just like – shit –

And people were bleeding from the broken glass, covered in dust, and everybody was just – *shocked* kind of isn't the word – they were like really *wired* and breathing really fast and just acting strange and shaking and –

And this one woman was screaming, so me and this other girl tried to calm her down.

And everybody wanted to get the fuck out of the office – run for the hills, you know – but the facilities guys were all like Stay Where You Are It's Not Safe to Leave the Building.

And part of me was like – fuck that, who listens to the *facilities* guys? Wearing a yellow Day-Glo fucking *tabard* doesn't make you the King of the World, you pompous, megalomaniac, fuck-stick cunts – but part of me knew they were probably right –

So I brushed the glass off my desk – by now I was sort of on autopilot, you know – trying to re-normalise my situation.

And I sat there at my desk, covered in dust and glass – trying to do the deep breathing from my yoga, but it wasn't helping in the *slightest* – and so I did what millions of other people were probably doing that exact moment – I googled 'Explosion, London', and pretty much within two seconds I just found this photo of – well, this woman, lying face down in the street, in this pool of –

She was in a really bad way. Like the bottom half of her was just – gone – sorry.

That was like five minutes after it happened.

She was outside the Space.NK apothecary on the New King's Road.

And all the hair on my arms was standing up because –

I was like – it fucking *can't* be.

But in my heart I knew it was.

And the one thing I'll always – my first reaction wasn't grief or – it was *disgust*.

Which I'm so unbelievably ashamed about. Thinking that. About my mum.

ANA *comes on, in a wheelchair. She should be wearing a roll-neck jumper or something, to hide her scars.*

They're not apparently aware of each other, but they are of us.

ANA. That morning – Friday 22nd July 2016 – I was on Eel Brook Common in Fulham – it was about ten-thirty. My shift at Strada didn't start until midday, but I'd arrived early so I could do some sunbathing. I was in a bikini, lying on a towel, reading a book.

And you know? It was the most beautiful day. The first day without rain for like a month. The sky was so blue.

And suddenly there was this *enormous* bang. It was louder than anything I've ever heard – louder than *reality* –

And I thought it was a car crash or a – I don't know – I
looked up – and –

Your mind can't *process* what you're seeing, it – this jumbo
jet plane *hurtling* straight at us – me – it was smashing the
trees in the park like matches as it – the whole plane flipping
over and over like this –

And it just smashed into the line of houses at the end of the
park –

And after it crashed I remember a split second where
everything was quiet – totally quiet – and then there was the
explosion, and then I was covered in burning aviation fuel –

And then I passed out.

FLOSS *joins them, apparently unwillingly.*

FLOSS. So I'm not sure what I can actually add to the whole –
I'm just not completely down with *emoting*, you know? Like
this. Feels a bit – dickish – a bit sort of *competitive*.

Sorry.

Fuck it. So basically I was in my dad's kitchen making a
sandwich and then all of a sudden this guy, still in his airline
chair, just crashed into the garden.

Wee – Bop.

Like a cartoon – a really fucking dark Tim Burton cartoon or
something.

And I – for the first couple of seconds he was alive, and then
he wasn't.

And I'm a twat, and I'll feel guilty for this for the whole of
my life, but the first thing I thought was just – that song –
'It's Raining Men!'

Sorry.

GRAHAM *enters.*

GRAHAM. I'm Graham. Welcome.

So to start off with tonight I'll just stick to the facts, right –
because some of what I'm going to be talking to you about,

it's right at the edge of what it's *possible* for me to talk about, yeah?

You get me?

So the SA-24 is a Russian man-portable infrared surface-to-air missile – it looks, you know, like a bazooka – put it on your shoulder, Blat! Flies at over eight hundred miles an hour, knocks a plane out of the sky at sixteen thousand feet.

So BU21 had no chance.

And, since the wars in Ukraine and Syria an SA-24 is now *ridiculously* easy to get hold of – well, if you're like a mentalist terrorist organisation with a decent amount of money, that is. I'd struggle to pick one up in the pub, you know?

Anyway – two guys. One drives the van to this industrial estate near Vauxhall, nobody much about, the other guy gets out the back, puts the rocket on his shoulder, points it at a plane, whoosh, gets back in the van, drives off. They had it all on the CCTV – forty seconds. Piece of piss. You don't even need to *aim* it.

The missile hits the plane somewhere over the river at Battersea Bridge, huge explosion, and it just smashes into Parsons Green, taking out a tonne of houses on the way.

I mean, what kind of a cunt would do that?

CLIVE *joins them.*

CLIVE. Hi. I'm Clive. Nice to meet you.

The trouble with stories is you never know how far to go back, do you, to make stuff make sense? Or is that just me?

Look – I'll just tell it from the very start so you can make your own decisions, okay?

So I was only like six or something when September 11th happened – and I literally had *no idea* what country New York was in, let alone who al-Qaeda were, or what jihadism was – but the next day – bang – I get punched in the face at school.

And I'm like – wow, what was that for?

Boy called Caius. Little shit. Classic class bully – you know? Thick neck, head like a football, bit like this – (*Mimes stupid face.*)

Probably in prison now –

Or a CEO or some shit, probably.

And from then on Caius called me 'Osama bin Clive'. Amazing mental journey he went on to reach that, you know?

And it was weird, because until then it hadn't *occurred* to me that there was even a *minimal* difference between me and everybody else in my class. We lived in the same sort of houses, our dads did the same sort of jobs, we watched the same stuff on TV, played with the same Transformers, everything. But after then, being a young Asian boy growing up in a mostly white area, every now and then – not *often*, I'm not trying to be whiney about it – but sometimes you're just like '*whoa* – are you actually being *serious*?' – especially after some terrorist shit's gone down recently.

I remember after the London Tube bombings when I was twelve – there was this *feeling*, you know? This *tension*.

Like all tension, though, you can kind of turn it to your advantage too? This one time, right, I was sitting on this packed bus next to a fat guy eating this really stinky skank-burger – it was really catching in my throat, like I was going to just vom on him –

So I just put my backpack on my lap –

And I close my eyes, put my hands out like this, and I start to mumble, like this – (*Mimes mouthing what sound like prayers.*)

Guy fucked off like a shot.

Whole seat for Clive, right there. Sweet as. Cheers, Osama.

So I wasn't even actually *praying* – that was the words to 'Bohemian Rhapsody' – Queen? (*Does it again – it is now clearly 'Bohemian Rhapsody'.*)

At that time I didn't even know any Muslim prayers.

Which was actually the other massive problem in my life.

THALISSA. So my office is in Chelsea, and I just decided – I just got up from my desk, and I just thought, fuck it – and I just started running down the street towards Parsons Green, towards Mum.

After about a hundred yards I – high heels, you know? *Hate* them – I just threw them off, and I ran down the street barefoot, like a hundred miles an hour – like Usain Bolt or something.

When I got near, the police, the fire engines – it was just chaos – they were trying to stop people from going too near, but it was impossible, because the area was just so *big*. And when I actually got there – the New King's Road, Favart Road, all the roads off – Chipstead Street, Quarrendon Street – they just weren't there any more.

They were all gone.

I was looking around like this – and I'd lived in these streets my entire life and I had no idea where I was any more.

And I saw – I don't want to even –

People turned into – who'd fallen from the plane – some of them were just piles of – I don't want to say *meat*, because they were people –

Sorry –

I had to get to Mum. I suppose even though she was clearly [dead] – I just needed to be the one who looked after her.

But I couldn't get to her. I was barefoot and there was so much glass, and my feet were cut to pieces and this policeman was shouting at me, and I just sat down in all this rubble – and I remember the smell – burning rubber and plane petrol and burnt hair – because the smell is still there, to this day, in my nose – however much you try and get rid of it –

The whole thing was just so *unreal*.

It felt like being in a *film* – like it wasn't actually *happening* to me – but I was just *watching* it – rather than actually, you know, *experiencing* it.

But then this guy just started taking photos of me sitting there – news guy, paparazzi, you know – and I just snapped out of it – and I stood up, and I screamed something at him, and he just looks at me blankly, and then I just punched him in the face.

Because fuck him, you know – that was the worst moment in my life, right there – and he wanted to steal my grief and sell it to a newspaper for profit. Fuck that.

ANA. And when I came to I was in this indescribable agony – but this animal instinct, it just kicked in – and I just wrapped my towel around me, and I rolled around and around until the flames went out. But when I tried to pull the towel off again – bits of my skin and flesh were still stuck to it. I found that quite hard to accept.

It was actually a Mickey Mouse towel, and I remember feeling so *sentimental* about getting blood on Mickey, like I'd done something unforgiveable.

All around me – the explosion had basically incinerated everything and everybody in the park.

And I don't know whether it's a miracle or a curse, that the human body can *live* through so much –

There was this woman, about twenty-five, and the blast had ripped most of her clothes off, and her flesh was shredded all down this side, like pulled pork, and she was walking towards me – totally bewildered –

(*Quietly.*) Calling out for her child.

And whatever kept that woman alive – whether it was God or adrenaline or whatever – for a few more seconds before she died, long enough to know that her baby was dead, is evil.

Sorry, I don't think I should carry on like this – you don't need to know.

It won't do anybody any good.

ALEX *bounds on, sits on the corner of the stage.*

ALEX. So hey, I'm Alex, great to see you and all that.

Thanks for coming.

Before we start, I just want to make sure that we're totally
clear about the parameters here – to set and manage your
expectations, make sure we all know roles and
responsibilities. All that standard corporate project-
management shit.

So you've paid your fifteen quid, twelve if you're some kind
of a massive screaming pikey – and for that you kind of
expect – what's the best way to put this?

As far as I can tell this is essentially a financial exchange
where you've paid money to be entertained by a bunch of
horrific human suffering – which – if you think about it, is
kind of weird.

Kind of dark.

But I suppose entertainment's a business like any other.

So, if that's what floats your boat – yeah – I can totally give
you your dirty little pervo fix, yeah?

Right, try this fucker on – it's a fucking doozy, right.

If you like that sort of thing.

So my girlfriend and my best friend were killed. She was at
his flat on the Harwood Road. And they were fucking. And I
didn't know.

They found them a week later. Like those bodies, you know,
in Pompeii, or whatever. *Fused*, they said in the inquest.
Fused together.

My best mate and my girlfriend.

'Surprise!'

Retrospectively, of course, there were these clues. There
were spunk marks in the bed where we didn't habitually
leave spunk marks – there was his casual touching of her

arm and stuff in the pub – there was the fact that she was the happiest I'd seen her for years, and I was barely putting any fucking effort into the relationship at all –

But you see what you want to see, believe what you want to believe. You're like – 'Will and Tilly? No fucking way.'

And you're at work like ninety hours a week so you can't like *police* it – and envy is such a pointless emotion, you know?

And it actually made it easier to *mourn* them – the consolation that they were a pair of cheating cunts.

For that I'm profoundly grateful, actually.

That first night after work I literally had nowhere to go – no clothes, no toothbrush, nothing.

So a lot of us from work went out, got smashed – what else could we do? And I was all messed up, and I ended up back at this girl's, and I was a bit like – (*Mimes shaking.*) and she was like:

'What's wrong? Are you with someone or something?'

And I thought of the helicopter footage of the wreckage of Harwood Road on the news – and I was like –

'No, I'm absolutely not.'

And when it was over, I was sick.

I don't normally feel, well – guilt is such a non-productive emotion – and the girl went fucking mental about the vomit, because it was all over her sheets, and she was like 'that's Egyptian cotton, you prick, from the fucking White Company' – and I was like –

'I'll buy you a dozen sets of your shitty chav sheets if you just shut the fuck up about it, because my girlfriend died this afternoon.'

– and then she just went *spastic* – fucking hysterical, like I was a serial killer or something – and then I had to spend an hour pretending to her I made it all up, and that I didn't really have a girlfriend, and that she wasn't dead, which

actually made me feel better, even though I knew it was a lie
– and then I just fell asleep –

I literally didn't know what I was doing that night – I was
totally in shock.

Autopilot.

But then if I hadn't have done – I'd have been on the streets
that night – I had nowhere else to go – and in a crisis, you do
what you have to do, you know.

FLOSS. And I was just staring at the chair guy, like this – (*Eyes
wide open.*) and I remember my mind did this double-take
and I thought for a second that it was, in some insane way,
Stephen Hawking in his wheelchair, and I was like – I didn't
know he *flew* now, or made random house calls – go,
disability!

Anyway – he looked up at me, and he caught my eye for a
moment, and then he just died. The light just went out –
quietly, and softly – And the thing is, he looked so kind.

Pause.

And we had to move out of the house for a week, and when
we came back chair guy was gone, and they'd tidied
everything up as best they could, jet-washed everything, you
know – fucked up the whole garden, actually – but there was
still this gash in the grass, and on the wall behind there was
this black stain – which was like corpse juice or something.

Charming.

And for six months me and my dad ignored the black stain
on the wall with this sort of studied indifference – I love him
for that – we made no mention of it at all – stiff upper lip, all
that shit – but neither of us went out into the garden either.

And then one day I came back home, and the wall had been
painted white, and there was this trellis and like roses or
something planted against the wall, and the gash had this
chiminea over it.

And I missed the black stain on the wall, actually. Weirdly.

And when I went to the inquest to give my little spiel – it'll
go on for like four years or something, so it's awesome that
I've done mine already – and Chairy – The Man Who Fell to
Earth – his name was actually Sunny Mir – *Sunny Mir* –
which is such an awesome name – and he was forty-seven,
and he was a doctor from High Barnet.

I didn't say anything, in the inquest, about him still being
alive. His family were there and I didn't want them to – so I
totally bossed the inquest – smashed it –

I kept that between me and Sunny.

Our little secret.

CLIVE. The thing is my family was actually, like, *relentlessly*
secular – my dad's a cardiologist and basically this hard-line
Richard Dworkin-worshipping atheist guy – you know,
science has absolutely *all* the answers, religion is – (*Gestures
idiot face.*)

In my house, religion, and especially Islam, was sort of
patronisingly looked down on like it was for those *less
fortunate* in life – like believing in God was *downmarket* –
sort of like bingo or ITV or car-boot sales or something –

And because my grandparents are all dead, and my parents are
almost neurotically well integrated – you know, all the fervour
of the young first-generation immigrant, desperate to be more
English than the English – I'm talking *tweed*, man, the works
– I was in the weird position of not *quite* fitting into the culture
where I lived, but also being a *total* stranger to the culture
where the racists thought I should eff-off back to.

And I'm not like my dad. I love my dad but – I've always been
quite a spiritual person, you know? I was sort of turned off by
the *coldness* of his scientific outlook – it excludes a space for
love, and kindness, and human fallibility, and wonder, and
gratitude – basically everything that makes life worth living.

I think.

So when I was a teenager I kind of rebelled against my dad's
emotionless sort of truth, and I started going to the mosque,
you know?

I needed it. I really *needed* it, man –

Both to discover where I'd come from, and to work out where I was going to.

ALEX. So I was *totally* back to work the next day. Totally fucking RoboCopped it. Didn't tell fucking *anyone*. Bosh.

It's a fucking dog-eat-twat world, mate, especially at work – chink in the fucking armour is all it takes to get the – you know – that medieval war thing – spikey – halberd or something – in.

And then when all the sick jokes started coming – internet memes, comedy clubs, all that – practically the very next day –

And it turns out that if the plane had crashed in like a poor area of London it'd have been entirely tragic – but in a *posh* area, people find it a *tiny* bit secretly hilarious.

But you know what? I actually sort of found it massively *cathartic*, you know, all the rancid internet jokes and class hatred.

If you can fucking laugh at it, you can beat it, you know.

Is that true?

Fuck it – it's called a poignard. Long dagger thing that you stick between armour. That's what it's called. Not a fucking halberd.

Charlie's dad has a wall of them in his house. Great Hall. Totally castled up, Charlie's dad.

He's totally buried in the family chapel, Charlie.

Skills.

How's this going so far? Digging it? Getting off?

Good for you.

GRAHAM. I always fucking hated it around Fulham. Pretentious cunts, Hooray Henrys, women who call themselves Yummy Mummies, whereas in reality they're furious skeletons in gym kit, one missed meal away from the grave – cunts called *Geoffrey* driving Range Rovers. Abysmal people.

I suppose at least they're always getting their houses done – I drive for a building delivery firm, so I suppose middle-class vanity is what keeps it afloat – lofts and cellars and extended kitchens and shit –

But nobody wanted to see that shit happen. Not even in *Fulham*.

I was one of the first TV interviews, right? But you probably know that already?

It's kind of *iconic*, if I say so myself.

Half an hour after. Still in, you know, shock:

GRAHAM *is now 'on TV', just after the crash – or he behaves as if he is.*

The plane – it came down right here – right over there, you understand? I wasn't more than a hundred yards away.

Pause.

I tried to save as many as I could. I think I got to five or six. I don't know. I wish it could have been more –

Pause.

And you know something? Whoever did this, I've got a message for you, pal – we won't ever be beaten. Not by you, not by anyone – because we're Londoners, and we're shoulder to shoulder, forever. You get me?

(*Normal voice.*) And when you agree to do one, they ask you to do another, and another – and it just sort of snowballs with a momentum of its own that you're not really in control of –

Until you're like a fucking *celebrity* and sweet old biddies come up to you in Tesco and thank you for what you said, with tears streaming down their faces. Seriously, I've been hugged by more weeping old ladies than Tom Jones, you know?

Weird as.

FLOSS. So the passengers from BU21 fell from four thousand five hundred feet. It's totally unsurvivable, unless you fall into deep snow or something, and you're like miraculously, freakishly, lucky.

I looked it up on the internet – one guy in the Second World War fell out of a bomber from thirty thousand feet, fell into a pine tree and then into snow, survived, stood up, lit a fag, scratched his head and wandered off.

Probably to a bar to get totally bongoed, I'd imagine.

But mostly you've got no chance. So there was nothing I could have done, even if I was like a doctor or an ambulance guy – rather than just a gormless idiot holding a cheese sandwich –

You know something? According to the medical guy in the inquest, about seventy per cent of the passengers were alive and conscious as they fell four thousand five hundred feet through the air.

Dat's a real bastard of a statistic to drop on us, doc.

I looked that up on the internet – how long a fall from four thousand five hundred feet takes.

Twenty-two seconds.

(*Counts*.) One,

Two,

Three,

Four,

Five,

Six,

Seven,

Eight,

Nine,

Ten,

Eleven,

Twelve,

Thirteen,

Fourteen,

Fifteen,

Sixteen,

Seventeen,

Eighteen,

Nineteen,

Twenty,

Twenty-one,

Twenty-two.

…BANG.

And I keep wondering what was going through Sunny's mind on the way down –

I keep timing myself twenty-two seconds – like five times a day, obsessively – and I try to reconcile myself with, like, death, in twenty-two seconds.

On the stopwatch on my iPhone.

And it turns out I run out of things to say after twelve seconds.

(*Takes out iPhone, sets timer.*)

Thank you for the gift of life, thank you for my friends and my family, for all the amazing things I've done, and places I've seen, I hope nobody grieves for me too much and I hope to fuck this doesn't hurt too much.

You see? Twelve fucking seconds.

What do I do for the other ten?

Do I just go WEEE and enjoy the ride?

CLIVE. When I was growing up I was against the wars in Iraq and Afghanistan, not because I was a Muslim – but because I wasn't a massive psychotic warmongering fuckwit with mad eyes like Tony Blair.

Because I was a *decent* human being.

And I've got this natural British desire to root for the underdog, the little guy – but in Afghanistan and Iraq we were the big guy, the marauding bully, the over-dog, the Caius –

And me and my dad would argue – fucking hell would we argue – about the war, about everything –

And when you're a teenager, the more somebody opposes you, the further to the other end of the spectrum you go.

So I kind of became really quite devout. Just to piss off my dad, really. In retrospect.

I started going to the mosque every day – grew a shitty bum-fluff beard.

And because all my parents wanted for me was for me to get on, do well, play the game – be a lawyer, suburban-respectability shit –

I thought, fuck that, too. I was going to do something greater and purer and more noble with my life.

Something with a proper spiritual purpose.

I was going to change the world.

Scene Two

We're in a support group. Semicircle of chairs. ALEX,
THALISSA, FLOSS, GRAHAM, ANA.

ALEX. So work suggested – well, they fucking basically
insisted – or they said they'd fucking fire me – that I go to
like a support group – I mean, for fuck's sake, right? –
because I was smashing so much coke and booze that some
days I wasn't turning up until like eleven in the morning, and
when I did I was gibbering about being raped by dinosaurs
and shit –

So –

In the meeting I was totally Leonides, utterly fucking Sparta
– I was like 'I fucking *dare* you to fire me when my house's
just burnt down and my girlfriend's just been incinerated by
a falling plane. It'd be a PR fucking *holocaust* for you. You
can't fucking *touch* me, basically.'

And there were like six of them, and they just stared at me –
you know, like this –

And in the end there's no point in calling their bluff on it.
These HR cunts are fucking *cold*. Fucking – bankers, you
know?

And it turns out a survivors' group is literally the best place
in the *universe* to pull.

You give it all this 'I've been hurt real bad, baby' shit, and
then you look down all like this – (*Morose and wounded.*)

And then look up all hopeful – and then you're like,

'I've never met anybody who understands me' – pregnant
pause – 'and what I'm *going through*, like you,'

And then you try to force out some actual tears through your
actual eyes – squeezing one of your balls with your
fingernails through your trouser pockets works – and in like
ten minutes they're noshing you off, pretty much guaranteed.

Target-rich environment, man, the seriously traumatised.

Mental.

THALISSA. So about a month after the crash I went back to
     work – but it turned out to be a massively shit decision
     because I was getting all these flashbacks and –

Well, everybody was being so *amazingly*, like *emphatically*
     kind and patient – but in my mind it was – because they were
     treating me like I was some sort of ticking time bomb –
     people would just talk to me. Really. Slowly. And.
     Concerned – like I was retarded or foreign or something –

And in the end I was in this client chemistry meeting and I
     stood up – in front of the senior client and everything – and I
     was just like – 'fuck's sake, can everybody *please* just stop
     being so fucking *kind* to me?'

And the account director just looks at me open-mouthed, and
     I ran out and just *hid*.

So here I am. And I've got to say, it's been totally fucking
     brilliant.

I mean, of course it's a *bit* cringe, but I'm a very *people-*
     person, and I'm very happy to be open and inclusive and –
     it's a cliché, but a problem shared really is a problem halved.

Some of the people are great.

There's this guy, Alex, a banker, at the group. To start with
     he was all like, you know, macho alpha-male dickhead – but
     underneath, I could just *feel* that he was as vulnerable as me.

I've just got this radar for people, you know.

And then one night we went for a drink together, and he just
     opened up to me. It was actually really beautiful.

He said that he'd never met anybody like me, anybody who
     understands him like I do – and I was like – me too, Alex.
     Me too.

And then we – well – she shoots, she scores!

That night was the first night that I'd felt happy in a long,
     long time.

FLOSS. So I was getting kind of teary at weird points, like at
     dinner and stuff – like there was something spontaneously

tragic about carrots – which isn't me at all – and my dad totally can't deal with that kind of nonsense, and so he was like – (*Ultra-posh voice*.)

'Um, you know, uh – I asked Cecily' – his secretary – 'to, see if there was anything that could be done about your' and he gestured forward in the air, in this vague way, bless him – 'and she's booked you into this, I'm sure it's a waste of time – 'and handed me a leaflet like this, like it had shit on it.

Which was so sweet of him I almost cried – but I didn't, obviously –

And I turned up the next week –

And the first thing I thought was that it was a little bit like a sort of *maimed* version of *Friends*, you know?

(*Sings*.) *I'll be there for you,*
Though we're torn limb from limb.

Sorry.

It was kind of worse than I was letting on. I just couldn't stop seeing Sunny. Everywhere.

Like literally I'd be walking down the street and suddenly out of the corner of my eye I'd catch sight of Sunny in the crowd, or in reflections in shop windows – or like he'd go past on a fucking bus when I was riding my bike.

It was fucking terrifying. The PTSD guy – Derek – of *course* he's called Derek – told me not to be scared of it – that it was perfectly normal for somebody who'd gone through what I'd gone through – but fuck's sake –

I mean what was I supposed to do, go:

'Oh, hi, weird corpse flashback. How *you* doing?'

'Yeah fine, dead and stuff. You?'

'Yeah fine, just having this massive psychotic episode – you know, seeing *you* and stuff – '

And then the lights would change and the bus would drive off.

I mean – I stopped looking in mirrors in case I saw him over my shoulder –

It was like a horror film – a really low-budget, shit, British horror film, that just kept going on and on and –

And I was kind of trying to get a handle on it – it mostly happened in busy, you know, restaurants and on Tubes so – so I just spent a lot of time chilling at the crib, word?

Didn't go out. At all.

And I was like – fuck, Floss, you're turning into a crazy psycho cat woman, you know? With all bats in your hair and shit? Postmen going like this – (*Shocked face.*)

When I answered the door?

I'd be like, come on, get up, you haven't worn outside clothes for a week now.

But then I'd be like – fuck me, is that *Countdown*? And I'd just sit down again, because I was so scared.

It was mental. And I mean *actually* mental.

This place is fucking jokes, man – seriously, the average conversation is like:

THALISSA. So, you still seeing a dead Pakistani guy on public transport, hun?

FLOSS. And I'm like:

(*Modestly.*) 'Yeah, *hun.*'

THALISSA. Yeah, so I pretty much constantly see the naked corpses of mutilated babies hanging from trees.

FLOSS (*to her*). I been there, sister.

(*To us.*) It's always great to meet people with similar interests to yourself, I suppose.

GRAHAM. So *my* main problem after 22/7 was rage. I had a lot of rage. I mean a LOT. Some of it was directed towards the numpties in MI5 and the police and the retards at the Channel Tunnel who missed a van with a five-and-a-half foot long *missile* in the back – I mean, it's not like a pair of fucking nail scissors in your hand luggage, is it? It's a cunting *missile*, you cunts.

But most of it was just like *outrage* – how *dare* these dirty fucking fuckers do this to *us*, to London?

Because these Muslim fuckers needed to be taught a lesson, you know? Death and violence is the only thing these people understand, and thank fuck the government did what they did – ignore the Twitter-hashtagging *Guardian*-reading fucksacks, the scruffy student candlelit peace vigils with their 'Not in My Name' shit – and they properly stepped up to the plate and – smashed it –

Globally trending hashtag 'We're All Londoners' – fuck *off*.

(*Wanker gesture*.)

So were the two terrorists. 'Londoners.' From fucking Bermondsey. That was the fucking *problem*. Should never have been allowed to be Londoners in the first place.

Newspapers said that the bombing raids were so severe that they picked them up on those seismic – you know, the earthquake machines? All across the world, you could pick the bombing up on the Richter scale.

And I don't want to be a cunt about it, but basically, I think the whole *Islamaphobia* thing is just a bit –

In the Second World War, right, we fought the Nazis – and nobody was accusing us of being *Nazi-phobic*, were they?

That would have been completely insane.

Yes, I'm against people who shoot down airlines onto cities, just like I'm against people who gas Jews in concentration camps.

I'm against evil people who do evil shit.

But this place, there's just this – (*Puts two fists together.*)

Unity, you know? London is basically made up of groups of people who hate each other: rich people versus poor people, immigrants versus locals, North London versus South

London, Arsenal versus Chelsea – but when the crash happened, for a moment, all of that stopped.

And for a second we were shoulder to shoulder. United.

I'm really fucking proud – of us all. Apart from the Muslims. They can fuck off.

And after a couple of months there was this Romanian girl, Anna – Ana, Ayna or whatever – joined the group – and I've never been a fan of East Europeans but – she was a waitress. And she'd been terribly burned. And the two of us just – I cried my fucking eyes out every night, thinking about what she'd gone through.

She was just so brave, and dignified – and she could barely move, she was in so much pain all the time – and in my heart I was just like 'you're as much a Londoner as I am, my darling, no matter what nightmarish gypsy-infested fuckhole you're from' – I'd have hugged her, only I didn't dare, what with her injuries.

And over the months we became close, me and her.

And every time I went home – and I'm not being funny – my heart was just *full*.

ANA. So I spent nine weeks in hospital in the end. Two of them I was in an induced coma.

A month after the crash I broke up with my boyfriend. He'd been visiting every day – every *single* day – but –

He's twenty-four. I didn't want him having to look after a cripple in a wheelchair for the rest of his life. It wouldn't have been fair.

If you love people, sometimes you've got to set them free –

Which I think is probably a line from like *Free Willy* or something – which means you probably shouldn't accept it blindly as a philosophy for life – but in this case, you know –

I'll have to have operations for the next five years. I've had twenty already this year.

He was broken-hearted, but hearts heal quick enough.

Faster than burns, it turns out, you know?

Now I've only got me to worry about, and I never worry about myself.

Never. Because I'm strong. Always have been. Nothing gets to me. Ever.

I come here every week now, to this group.

Obviously it's a waste of time.

As if you can *talk* what happened to me away?

I mean, you can't set a bone with sympathy, can you? Stitch a wound with concern? So it's naive to think you can heal my mental injuries that way, isn't it?

The people are kind, I guess. Kinder than they used to be around here.

When I was waitressing there, in Fulham – it was so unreal for me – I used to walk past the estate agents, and the house prices were more than everybody I know will ever earn in the whole of their lives put together – and sometimes the customers would, you know, make these arrogant jokes that I had to pretend to laugh at – and their children often behaved very poorly and I had to pretend to laugh at that too – and people were often rude in this *offhand* way, like I was this *bug* or something – so it wasn't always a happy time for me.

But since the crash – there seems to be a little more feeling of solidarity, I think. A little less division.

Of course there are some people you don't – like anywhere – there's this lorry driver who is just this patronising, bigoted, *absurd* man –

But some of the others, you know – they're not so bad.

CLIVE *comes onto the stage. He stays away from the rest of the group.*

CLIVE. Of course I regret what happened. I'm not a total fucking –

A couple of years back I'd got a place at Warwick to study law – I was going in October that year –

And I was home one night, watching telly, and on the news there was this film of these kids, in Syria, that Assad had gassed. You know the film? Kids, man. Who the fuck gasses kids? Cunts.

And for me, that was the thing. This guy was a fucking cunt and he was gassing kids. And I wasn't going to stand for it any longer. Something in my mind just went snap. I was going to go. To help. Not to fight, necessarily. To *help*.

This is before ISIS was such a massive thing, you know – where that choice was still a realistic possibility –

And by then things were really shit with my dad – and we were arguing every night, pretty much – and I thought – fuck it – let's put aside our differences – let's do this as an *us* thing.

And I said to him – 'Dad, let's go *together*. You and me. Let's go and help. You're a doctor, and I can help you as, like, a stretcher-bearer or something.'

And he just looked at me. Like I had tentacles or something.

And I was like – 'Dad. These people need our help. Fellow Muslims, Dad. People dying. They need medics. I – '

And I just look at him, imploring.

And he went mental. Totally freaked out. He was just screaming that I was a simpleton, that he hadn't raised a son to die as a suicide bomber, that he was ashamed of me –

He may be a doctor, but he certainly isn't a fucking psychologist, is he?

And he forbade me from going, and we both got really, really worked up – and I said some things that I regret – really regret – to this day.

And things changed between us.

But in the end, of course, I did what he said – I'm a pussy – my parents just piled and piled this pressure on me – totally rubbed me fucking out –

So I went to university, stayed in the UK, but I massively resented it, and him. I'd make excuses not to come back during the holidays, all that stuff. Hated him.

And then one day my mum turns up at the restaurant where I'm waitering for the summer, and she tells me that Dad's died in a plane crash on his way back from a cardiology conference in New York.

It tears me to pieces, the fact that we never made it up, me and Dad.

Tears me to fucking pieces.

FLOSS. And then one week I go in, sit down, and Derek says hi, and we say –

ANA/GRAHAM/FLOSS. Hi, Derek.

FLOSS. And he starts going on and on in his passive-aggressive little Napoleon way about biscuits – literally, biscuits in group-therapy groups assume this fucking *insanely disproportionate* significance – like they stand for everything you've lost –

(*Derek voice.*) *Have as many biscuits as you like.*

(*Rolls eyes.*) But every time you actually take one he looks at you like you're a serial killer and you're ripping his baby's heart out and eating it in front of his face.

True say.

Anyway, we're in the middle of this absurd introductory-biscuit shit for the millionth time, and I look up – trying to catch Becks' eye to – you know – roll our eyes –

And all of a sudden I just literally –

(*Can't continue.*)

And I thought that I'd finally lost my mind, and I'd gone, you know, psychotic for ever, and I start shaking, really shaking, and I can feel the sick in my throat and all this adrenaline is just –

Because Sunny fucking Mir is sitting in the seat, just there, in a fucking hoodie, next to Ana the Roasted Romanian, and Alex the Priapic Banker, and he looks up at me, and he's like –

CLIVE *sits down next to* FLOSS.

CLIVE. You must be Florence.

FLOSS (*very agitated*). What the fuck? Get the fuck away from me –

CLIVE (*confused about this reaction*). Florence? I'm really sorry I –

FLOSS (*shouting*). Just get the fuck away from me.

CLIVE. Florence!

She runs out. Followed by CLIVE.

ALEX. And so Derek the pencil-dicked psychologist chases them out, but they're gone, and we carry on for a little bit, but it's all a bit weird.

Oh, and, by the way, you guys – classic – you're fucking racists, yeah?

Brown guy? Must be a terrorist.

Who knew theatre audiences were so fucking BNP, man? I thought you were all supposed to be champagne socialists? But *Sieg* fucking *Heil*!

Anyway, we'll come back to Floss and the dead guy later. For now let's check in on some suffering.

Come on, I'm going to narrate this shit properly:

(*With an ironic* Jackanory *edge*.) 'So the months have passed, and some of our support-group members are dealing with their heavy hearts and wounded limbs with courage and plucky determination.

'Others amongst our number, sadly, are finding it harder to bear the burden of their pitiless tragedy.'

You like that shiz? Anyway, a lot of what they chat about is just a circle-jerk of self-indulgent misery-porn, but you might just learn some shit from *some* of it.

(*Game-show-presenter voice*) *Let's give it a go.*

THALISSA (*to the group*). Hi, everybody.

ANA/GRAHAM. Hi.

THALISSA. So Mum's funeral went off better than expected.

My sister's in events management, so, you know – professional touches – I don't want to call it *slick*, because it was a – but it was, you know – well executed.

It was Mortlake, you know, Crematorium. Horrible 1950s building, looks like a telephone exchange.

It's next to a recycling centre. Which I suppose is some kind of sick town planners' joke.

Dicks.

There's the most amazing rose-garden thing at the back – and there was this old gardener there, like he'd been there for like a hundred years, and I was going to ask him how on earth they did so well with them – but then I looked at the earth and kind of realised – ah – human ashes.

Nice.

And during the service the priest, who didn't know her at all, was busy making my mother into this heroic, saintly, you know – based on the scant biographical details provided by my sister in a bullet-pointed email the day before – and I saw it there, the coffin, and it seemed like some kind of ridiculous joke.

Her broken body, just there. My mum.

And what made it so very raw was that – the plane engine had bounced down the King's Road and it'd killed only her. There'd been dozens of other people on that street. But it'd killed only *her*.

Like God was out to get her.

Or was just really shit at bowling, I suppose.

You know, it's not like I'd have wanted *more* people to be killed by it, obviously, but the fact it was *just* her – it made me angry with the priest, and what he stood for. Like God should have prevented it from happening – not that I even believe in God –

And I know that's irrational and stuff, and I expect you're judging me for it but –

ANA. Of course we're not judging you.

GRAHAM. I think what you've just said is the bravest thing I've ever heard and – I'm sort of welling up here.

ALEX (*to us*). What do you reckon? I mean, I'm fucking her, so I'm probably biased, but to be frank, I sort of had to stop myself laughing at one point there –

I even went to the funeral. Her sister's *vastly* hotter than her – but cracking onto your girlfriend's younger sister at their mum's funeral – I kind of draw the line there –

Or would that be the most legendary pull of all time?

Anyway – try this – which was the next up –

GRAHAM. Thanks, everybody, for being here today, and for continuing to be so supportive.

ANA. Hi, Graham.

THALISSA. Hi, Graham.

GRAHAM. So yesterday I went back to Fulham for the first time. I felt I was ready. It was hard. I can't pretend it wasn't hard.

They were winching the nose of BU21 out of the park. Putting it on the back of a lorry.

It was just so fucked – sorry for swearing – a crazy ball of twisted metal, wires like blood vessels or something hanging out everywhere – dried mud and tattered seat fabric.

You could see the seats inside. With these stains on them.

You know – blood and stuff.

There were a lot of people there, outside the fuck-off wooden walls they'd built around the crash site.

I was right at the front.

And when it drove through the streets, the nose, surrounded by all the police motorbikes and stuff – it was the last big piece of the plane – they were taking it to a massive hanger for the investigation –

And the crowds were just silent. Like nothing I'd ever seen. And the tension was fucking palpable.

Like the air was going to explode.

And then this one woman starts clapping.

(*Claps*.) And then somebody else, and another –

And I don't know what the fuck they were clapping for – and I was thinking a bit like – shut the fuck up, you fucking bitch –

And then everybody was.

And then I was too.

And it was –

It was the most beautiful thing I've ever seen in my entire life.

(*Breaks down*.)

THALISSA (*somewhat wearily*). We're here for you, Graham.

ANA. Yes, we're here for you.

GRAHAM. Thanks, darling –

He goes to hug ANA. *She bristles. He doesn't.*

GRAHAM. Yeah, I'll just – (*Gestures to sit down*.)

ALEX. Graham, the grinning moron on every Union Jack tea towel in *Daily Mail* land.

So, so far, I'm not sure I'm finding any of this cathartic, to be honest. I'm not sure I'm learning anything. It's just like people talking about being unhappy – and I'm like, what's that to me?

What about you? How you finding it? Good?

But then there was this – from Ana – who to be honest, I actually sort of respect.

I sort of bet she was even a little bit hot before – the meds make you puffy –

I wonder how much of her is actually, like, scarred? Under that jumper?

That'd be a night to remember – down by the fireside, tipping her out her wheelchair onto the sheepskin rug…

Look, just because she's disabled, that doesn't mean you should exclude her from being a sexual being, okay?

You guys are fucking prejudiced, okay?

ANA. So I've stripped my life back to basics, you know? I've cut out everything I don't need.

My day is now much simpler and more manageable, because I just eat, sleep, and control my pain.

I don't even watch the TV any more. So many of the programmes were, you know, about BU21 –

It's like maths. Limiting the variables.

My mother and father phone me every single day. On Skype, you know.

They ask me how I'm doing – check in. They can't afford to fly over, and planes are kind of not great for me –

So I invent a lot of things I'm doing. I say 'tonight I'm going out for drinks with people from my old work' or 'yesterday I went on the pedalos in Hyde Park with a friend' –

And they inevitably ask – 'boy or girl' and I pretend to be all coy.

I tell them I've got job interviews. They tell me not to push myself too hard, and to concentrate on getting better first.

I tell them 'you know me, can't just sit around the house all day!'

Of course none of it's true.

I don't want them to worry.

When I'm telling the stories, I'm actually enjoying them, in real life, like they actually happened.

Because the life that I've invented for myself is fun, you know?

I think maybe they don't always believe the stories, but they need to hear the *fiction* of my happiness as much as I do.

Because the truth is, it's not always so good.

ALEX. And she's right.

When something like this happens, you spend all your time escaping from the truth –

You create yourself an alternative reality – one that's liveable.

This support-group shit – it's fucking nonsense.

I mean, it's clear than Derek goes back every night and boshes one off over every misery-porn story –

(*Porn accountant voice.*) *Oh yes, oh yes, oh yes, have as many biscuits as you like. I've jizzed on all of them, you little sluts.*

(*Normal voice.*) Seriously, I never touch the lemonade. A little bit too cloudy not to have spunk in it. Just sayin'.

So yeah – if your life has been torn to pieces, build yourself a new one.

Step the fuck up.

It's fucking simple as. Don't *whine* about it, *change* it.

So Thalissa and I are moving in. Together.

Three-bedroom mews house off the Fulham Road. Her dad paid, obviously.

She's grieving and desperately vulnerable, and *I* have nowhere to live and very few scruples.

Match made in heaven.

Yeah, I know.

She's – well – (*Makes so-so gesture.*)

No, she's good, you know?

Her father's a partner at Goldman. Massive guy to know in case things ever go Hiroshima at work.

Ghastly fucking wonky tits on her though. Like the left one's had a stroke or something.

Tilly had the most perfect tits. Like a fucking Canova sculpture.

Turned out they were glazed in Will's spunk, whenever I wasn't looking, but you know –

The point's still valid.

But there's no point getting too worked up about it, is there, because they're both just ashes now, aren't they?

They're gone.

I don't think about them. I train myself.

And if you think that sounds inhuman, that 'feelings are what makes you human' –

Then fuck off, you're being a twat –

Because to cope, you've got to become a creature that's no longer fully human.

(*Snaps out of it.*) Doing well at work, you know?

Everybody's fucking caning it now, after the initial crash – (*Hollow laugh.*)

Stock-market crash.

Massive growth in construction and infrastructure firms, defence procurement, lawyers and other allied professional-services entities, healthcare – the list goes on and on.

And, as Baron Rothschild said, 'When there's blood in the streets, buy property.'

Quite literally.

Everybody's making a killing, you know?

Sorry.

And, to be even *more* brutal about it, a lot of bankers died in Fulham, so my promotion prospects are, you know – 'rosy'.

So actually, today, I'm kind of in a much better position than I was before. I'm totally beasting it.

Lucky me.

Anyway, back to Floss.

Scene Three

The chairs are gone, we're in another space on the stage.

CLIVE. So I ran down the King's Road, trying to find Florence.

And I was bashing into people, tapping these random girls on the shoulder –

So it turns out that trying to find a posh blonde girl on the King's Road is literally fucking impossible – they *all* look identical from the back – skinny jeans, ponytail, gilets – I don't even know how they tell *each other* apart.

But I couldn't find her.

And I *had* to find her – because when I'd gone to the inquest, my dad's inquest, she was there, giving evidence.

My dad died in her back garden, you see.

And because of that I knew her address and her name, and I just found out from her Facebook that she came to these PTSD things here – and I –

I wasn't going to tell her all that, obviously – because that sounds fucking stalkery –

Which I'm not – well –

I was going to tell her that it was all more *coincidental* than that.

But she told the story in the inquest so beautifully, with so much compassion and tenderness –

More tenderness than I was ever able to have with my dad, you know?

I don't know *what* I wanted, but I kind of knew that I had to talk to her.

And I knew that *somehow*, us meeting was fated.

Divine providence.

FLOSS. So I'm in my street, just getting to my house, and fuck's sake, if it's not the effing corpse again, running down the road like a – you know – bat out of hell or something.

The days you're out without your crucifix and your stake, you know?

But this time I was just like – fuck it. I was sick of it. I just was like –

(*To* CLIVE.) *Come on then. If you want a piece of me, here I am, you know?*

CLIVE (*to* FLOSS). I'm sorry?

FLOSS (*to us*). And I kind of looked at him, and I was kind of confused because it *was* Sunny and it kinda *wasn't*.

And he was totally going to say something – he was all – (*Poised to speak.*)

And then he kind of wimped out, and almost turned around to go –

And then all of a sudden he just blurted out –

CLIVE (*to* FLOSS). I'm sorry I was chasing you. I'm really not a psycho, it's just my dad died in your garden and I kind of wanted to see where he – but if that's, like, not convenient... Sorry.

FLOSS (*to* CLIVE, *bewildered*). Fuck.

CLIVE (*quietly, apologetically*). I'm really not a psycho.

FLOSS (*to us*). So, as a general rule, I find that if a stranger opens a conversation with 'I'm really not a psycho – ' best thing is normally to run for the hills because they're total batshit, but – I've never been any good at following advice, especially my own.

She sizes him up.

(*To* CLIVE.) Fuck it, do you want to come in and have some coffee?

CLIVE (*to us*). And that was it – the mood just – thawed – she let us in, with her keys on this key ring with a panda on it – it was enormous – oil paintings, massive bookshelves, dozens of invitations on the mantelshelf – it was fucking amazing.

And I thought back to Dad's house in High Barnet – the new furniture, the electric gate, the massive flat-screen TV, and I was suddenly mortified by how *nouveau riche* we were – like it was kind of *gauche* that my dad, the Pakistani immigrant, died in her garden – I can't explain it.

Fuck it –

And we went in, and she took me to the garden.

FLOSS (*to* CLIVE). So, here we are.

CLIVE. Yes. Was it here?

FLOSS. More, kind of, here.

CLIVE. Oh.

FLOSS. Although there was some there too.

(*Apologetically.*) Shit, sorry.

CLIVE. No worries.

FLOSS. You could kind of see more where it was before, but my father had the wall repainted and a chiminea put over the hole left by the seat.

CLIVE. Yeah. You'd kind of have to do that, wouldn't you – tidy everything up. Get things back to normal –

FLOSS. It wasn't like that – Dad, he just –

CLIVE (*with difficulty*). Look. I just wanted to say sorry on behalf of the whole family for all the trouble it caused you.

FLOSS (*to us*). And the guy's dad was dead, and all he wanted to do was apologise for the mess. The sweet, sweet little fucker. And I was all like –

(*To* CLIVE.) Don't be ridiculous. Honestly, it was no trouble at all –

(*To us*.) And then I wanted to just *die* – 'it was no trouble' – what a massive *tool* – like it was his dog that shat in the garden rather than –

(*To* CLIVE.) Let's move the chimenia so you can see properly – if you want?

CLIVE. I'd like that.

FLOSS. Look, here, let me –

She offers to move it, bending down in the process.

CLIVE. No, seriously, let me. It looks heavy.

FLOSS. We can do it together?

CLIVE. No, seriously, I can manage if – I don't want you to fuck your back –

FLOSS. Quite.

(*To us*.) And it was sort of getting to be this weird Mexican standoff –

(*To* CLIVE.) I'll go and make some coffee, yeah?

CLIVE. Thanks.

She leaves.

(*To us.*) What the fuck do I do now?

(*Looks around.*) I'm not going to move that fucking chimenia, for starters.

I didn't want to seem like a pussy in front of her – but fuck me, I'm as weak as a kitten at the best of times, man –

And this is the place where my dad died – and the only thing I can think of is that when she bent over I definitely saw her bra strap –

And I looked at the spot in the ground where Dad died, and I bent down and I touched it, because I sort of thought that's probably what you should do in this sort of situation – sorry, Dad – I didn't have a plan, you know –

(*Does this.*)

And then I was a bit like, okay, I thought that would be a bit more, like, poignant and moving, but it's just some grass and – (*Takes a deep breath.*)

Bye, Dad. I'm glad I saw this place. I feel closer to you here than I have for a long time.

I know we didn't always get on, but I fucking loved you, okay?

FLOSS *returns.*

FLOSS (*to us*). And when I came back he was just looking so *lost* – and *kind*, like his dad –

And I thought about telling him about Sunny, and how kind *he* looked as he died, but I couldn't, and then we sort of looked at one another, and neither of us knew what to say, so I told him that he could come back to the garden whenever he wanted, of course he could –

CLIVE. I don't even know *what* I was thinking – I just had this rush of blood to the head I guess.

It's just that, all of a sudden, after months of being so fucking unhappy, I suddenly felt joy and happiness surging back into my broken fucking heart – and I suddenly understood: love is the answer to everything, the cure for everything, the meaning of everything –

I felt free. For the first time in my life – and it was glorious, man. It was what I'd always lacked.

But I should never have tried to kiss her.

He goes for the lunge.

FLOSS. When you're about to kiss a boy there are two basic questions –

One: Do you fancy him?

Two: Is now a good time?

The guy was doing *so-so* on being hot –

And – when you're so depressed you're not going out of the house, you kinda stop shaving your legs – so it wasn't a great *time* –

But to this I'll add a third:

Three: Does he precisely resemble a corpse from your nightmares?

And it was mostly the third point – 'the corpse protocol' – that I really wasn't going to let slide, to be honest.

So he was leaning over, like that – (*Mimes somebody wanting to be kissed.*)

And I was like:

(*To* CLIVE.) What the *fuck*?'

CLIVE (*crushed*). I'm so sorry. I should go.

FLOSS. It's not you, it's – (*Points at the ground.*)

You know?

CLIVE. Of course.

FLOSS (*to us*). And he looked at me with this *despair* – and there's been quite enough of that shit going down in this city already, you know?

And I was sad and vulnerable – probably the most vulnerable I'd ever been – and I kinda wasn't thinking straight – but I kinda knew I really had to get the images of Sunny out of my fucking head, and maybe this – maybe this would help me exorcise them – who knows – maybe I just deserved to live a normal life again now – and maybe this would help –

But you know what? There are times in your life where you've just got to *not* think, just fucking – commit –

And then I just kissed him.

Fuck it.

She does.

Scene Four

ANA *alone in her wheelchair.*

ANA. Three months later, and I'm not getting any better. Physically, a little. Here – (*Points to her head.*)

Far worse.

I've stopped going to the group.

They tell you to discuss, to share, to 'have a dialogue' – but nobody who is suffering has a *dialogue*, ever.

Suffering *isolates* you from the world. It doesn't bring people together. How could it?

If you don't believe me, try putting your hand in the flames of a lighter, and then attempting to think about *anything else* than the pain.

Yes?

In the group, it was just people talking to themselves about their own suffering – caught up in their own pain to the complete exclusion of anybody else – monologue after monologue.

Suffering makes you so *selfish* – and I hate being selfish, but I can't stop suffering. So what can I do? What's the solution?

So today I went downstairs, but all the food in the fridge was rotten, the bread had mould on it – I hadn't gone out for twelve days by this point, probably, maybe two weeks – and I just knew that the only thing more rotten than any of this food – and more fit for the bin – was me.

And there were these Moshi Monsters yogurts in the fridge, and usually they made me smile – the ridiculous faces on them – you know – but today, I didn't feel anything –

And the sink was full of washing up, but I just couldn't – because nothing had any value, or purpose, or even emotion. Everything was just flat.

And I looked at my life, calmly and clearly. I weighed up the pain and the effort it cost me, versus the pleasure and the happiness I gained from it. And the outcome was clear. *Mathematically* clear.

My life simply wasn't worth living any longer.

GRAHAM *bounds onto the stage, full of purpose.*

GRAHAM. So I've got this amazing sense of purpose, these days.

I'm so fucking pumped up.

Basically, I got the idea a couple of weeks back. Whenever I saw my friends I started to notice that they almost always avoid mentioning BU21. Like it never happened. Which is fucking weird.

It's English, isn't it? Brush it under the carpet, you know –

If you walked down the street with a fucking unicorn's horn sticking out your forehead, everybody would be like –

(*English embarrassment.*) Ah – oh, look – what lovely roses!

It's not malicious, they're just trying to not bring up painful shit.

But it's like the most important event in my life just increasingly is edited out of my life.

Fuck that. That's why I'm writing the book.

Ta da! *BU21: The Survivors' Stories*.

I was *asked* to do it – it wasn't, like, *from* me – my agent said there were like twenty publishers fighting for my story.

But I don't want to focus just on *my* story.

I mean, I'm at the *centre* of it, but –

So what I'm also doing is doing little vignettes of other peoples' experiences too, you know?

And the PTSD group I go to – there are all these people with all these inspiring stories –

And every time I go, I go home and write down their stories, for the book.

Obviously in the book I'll mask their identities, you know – I'll call Alex 'Seb' or something, and instead of him losing his girlfriend he'll lose, I don't know, his *boyfriend* – give it a more modern angle, you know?

And Thalissa I'll change to her sister dying, not her mum – and change her name to like Ellie or something. Maybe her twin sister?

You know, to mask their identities, and to focus the story a little to make it more – more – I don't know –

Not *exciting* – that's ghoulish –

More 'resonant' – that's the word the publisher used.

Resonant.

And before I signed up I made it clear that a *proportion* of the money I get will go to the BU21 Survivors' Charity.

Fifteen per cent.

Which doesn't seem much – but fuck's sake – I mean, I'm actually *writing* the fucker – and I have to be reimbursed for my time, you know – because while I'm doing it, I'm not driving the van.

Well, there's a ghost writer who's doing a lot of the actual wordsmithing, you know – the keyboard-pounding.

It's actually the same guy who did all those SAS guys' books?

I can live with that.

You know what else? I'm doing a speech with the Prime Minister next month – well, he's going to be there – probably – at a rally for the 22/7 Action Group.

Boy done good, you know?

THALISSA *appears. She looks much more poised, more confident.*

THALISSA. So I'm definitely getting better, I think? Not moving on, but *moving*. Finally. I've always been this irrepressible optimist and –

So a month after my mum's funeral we just decided that we'd set up a charity in her name – the Polly Henderson Trust.

We were sitting around at dinner – my father, sister, and Alex – chatting about it.

We're like totally together now, me and Alex.

Utterly – (*Makes suitable gesture of closeness.*)

You know?

Sometimes adversity really –

It's just really great.

Sorry, I'm probably even blushing and stuff.

And my sister was all like – 'there've been so many charities set up because of this thing, how are we going to differentiate ours and stuff?'

And I do charity PR, so I'm well aware – it's a fucking crowded market.

You need a proposition that stands out.

What's *great* about our family is that between us, though, we can pretty much sort out anything –

We have the tools. We have the talent!

Seriously, though, we've got each other, it means we get through stuff.

And Soph was all like suggesting a charity that would rebuild that nursery on the King's Road – the one that –

You know – that one –

But Dad checked it on his iPhone, and there were already three charities just for that one nursery – they'll live like fucking kings, those kids – sorry – and we were like – (*Gestures frustration.*)

I mean, every single fucker in Fulham is endowing *something* or other – you're fucked if you can land a plaque on a fucking park bench, these days, let alone renaming a primary school or a hospital ward. Remembrance is getting fucking competitive.

So in the end we've endowed a home for seriously injured owls in Leicestershire – which wasn't really anybody's first choice, but it's a legacy for Mum, you know.

It's something.

ALEX *comes in. He sits on the edge of the stage, looks directly at us.*

ALEX. Yeah, ever tried to get owl shit out of a cashmere jumper? Fucking nightmare. Utterly should have wrung the little bastard's neck, but with owls, their heads go all the way round, don't they? So it's a fucker to actually. Wring. Them.

(*Mimes this.*)

They're all like – 'is that all you got, precious?'

(*Smiles.*)

Anyway, it was during the ceremony of dedication, so it would have been fucking poor form – I mean, the whole thing's set up to *preserve* the owls, not *massacre* them willy-nilly.

And he *knew* it, the little cunt.

Anyway, that's not important.

So, a month has passed since you last saw me, and to be totally frank with you I've just nailed a line of gack around the back so from now on, I'm totally, totally focused on the story, right?

Relentlessly focused on the story.

Oh, by the by, you've only got like fifteen minutes of this left now, so if you need a piss, hold it in, you're going to be fine –

And anyway, this is the best bit of the whole thing, by far, so lean the fuck in –

So, last week, this guy Graham – you know, chav media darling, rabble-rousing-cunt Graham – comes up to me afterwards and asks me whether I'd like to come for a drink with him.

(*Exaggerated East End voice.*) 'Cus I got something facking important to talk to you about, innit?'

He doesn't speak like that, but I can't do the voice, you know.

And so I say I'm busy, because he's clearly a *stratospheric* dick, but he insists – and in the end I'm like, whatever, *innit*?

ALEX *and* GRAHAM *arrange two chairs, so they're sitting opposite one another.*

ALEX. So he's knocking away his fizzy beer – ten-minute pints, like he's at a stag night or something – and he's going on about Regaining the Glory Days of England and Standing Shoulder to Shoulder Against the Forces of Evil – fucking drivel, you know –

And he tells me that the reason he invited me for a drink was to ask me whether he could use me as a featured 'case study' in the book that he's writing – and I'm like –

'Yes, mate, feel free to use the deeply personal and humiliating story of my dead girlfriend boffing somebody else, told to you in confidence in a mental-health group, to enrich yourself. Seriously, crack on.'

And he's like –

GRAHAM. Cheers, mate!

ALEX. And I'm like –

> (*To* GRAHAM.) *Mate*, you fucking mention anything about me in your book, even the merest hint or insinuation, and my lawyers will rip out your still-beating heart and show it to you before you die, alright?

> (*To us*.) And he's like.

GRAHAM. Suit yourself.

> *Beat*.

> What's that on your jumper?

ALEX (*to* GRAHAM). It's owl shit.

> (*To us*.) And then he's going on about the day of the crash, how he was just in Fulham by chance on a delivery, and how it changed his life, and how his interview gave people *hope* and *strength* – you know, his 'iconic' interview –

> I know, right? Chav Churchill demagogue bollocks to you and me – but the proles lap it up like nobody's business –

> And then he tells me how on his drive home he decided to dedicate his life to 'the cause' – and I suddenly realise something about him.

> Things suddenly fall into place.

> 'Your *drive* home?' I ask him. 'So where was your car parked?'

> And he was like.

GRAHAM. Just round the corner, mate.

ALEX. Which was weird because they didn't let anybody drive away that was within about a mile of the crash – outer cordon, you know – my Audi was fucking cordoned off for three weeks in Bagleys Lane –

> And I was like 'So where exactly were you when the plane crashed?'

> And he was like –

GRAHAM. I can't remember, mate – concussion, probably.

ALEX. And then he pauses and says –

GRAHAM. On the corner of the Wandsworth Bridge Road and the King's Road – I remember now, clear as day.

ALEX. And I told him that was weird, because, you know, that whole junction was completely and utterly destroyed, so he wouldn't have stood a chance if he was actually standing *there*.

And he's like umming and ahh-ing and saying he can't quite remember with the shock, and I ask him –

'So the five or six people you rescued – where *exactly* did you rescue them from?'

And he's floundering around –

And I just knew at that moment *for certain* that he was nowhere near the crash when it happened.

ANA. And I sat at the kitchen table with the carving knife in one hand, like this – and my other hand on the table.

And then I think for a second, I put the knife down, and I get up, and I get the bowl from the sink, the washing-up bowl, and I put that by my feet. The blood can go in there, because my housemates, they're cleaners anyway, they don't want to come back to more work, you know?

I think, okay.

Alright already. Piss or get off the pot.

And my father is an atheist, but my mother, she believes in God, goes to church, so I thought I'd pray, for her, before –

And I start:

She recites the first four lines of the Lord's Prayer in Romanian.

And I stop – because I can't for the life of me remember the second half of it.

And I think for a second, I put the knife down, and I go to google it on my phone.

And I'm about to unlock my phone, but the photo on the front, the wallpaper –

It's Mickey Mouse.

And I think back to the plane, and being in that park, and how the Mickey Mouse towel saved my life, and I look at Mickey – ridiculously happy, like he's on drugs, Mickey – and I think of when I was a child, and how I used to sleep every night with a Mickey Mouse soft toy, and how he's still in my parents' house in Bucharest, probably –

And all of a sudden I had this moment, this overpowering moment of truth – and I realise how ridiculous I must look – a washing-up bowl at my feet, checking the words to the Lord's Prayer in Romanian –

And all of a sudden I think it's so funny.

And I just start laughing.

And I just can't stop laughing –

And it turns to tears, the laughing –

But then it's laughing again.

And you know the total, absolute truth, right?

It wasn't God who saved my life that day.

It was Mickey fucking Mouse.

GRAHAM. So the truth of it is that I wasn't actually there.

Okay?

Not in the way that people, you know, imagine.

I wasn't there when it happened.

That morning I was helping out a mate on a painting and decorating job in Munster Road. Sanding down the filler, you know? And I was just getting in the van to go to Brewers for some more filler – Tetrion, you know – and I saw this plane – you know – about a mile or so in the distance, go down –

So I fucking motor down as fast as I can to see what's going on, but I get as far as the Fulham Road, and everything's fucked with the traffic. So I leave the van, and I run down to where the flames are.

My blood's really up, you know? Fucking pumped. Adrenaline.

This is about fifteen, twenty minutes after it had happened, by this point.

There were all these people coming towards me, scared shitless. People were just, you know, out of control. I got knocked down and I cut my head, and I didn't even feel it.

But I kept on going, because I wanted to see, you know, what was going on?

Everybody does it. When there's a crash on the motorway, everybody slows down to rubberneck shit. It's human nature. We're just made like that.

No, you know what? I take that back. I was going to *help* – in my mind, that was my definite fucking aim to *help* – but when I got there it was just, you know, chaos, and I was actually really, really frightened.

And I get closer and closer, but still I can't see anything because of all the police and firemen and shit –

And I was covered in all this white filler dust from sanding down the walls of the house in Munster Road – like a fucking ghost – and when I get to Harwood Road this ambulance driver takes one look at me and puts a foil blanket over my shoulders and walks me over to the triage thing by Fulham Broadway Station, telling me over and over that I'm going to be alright and shit.

And I didn't, like, stop him – I mean, I had a cut. Here. Little one. (*Points to his head, a little embarrassed.*)

I guess I just wanted to be a part of it.

I dunno.

And it's at this point that the TV crew comes up to me.

And it's not as if I was going to be all like, 'Yeah I just popped down to gawp at some dead bodies – alright, Mum!' – (*Does thumbs-up to camera.*) on national TV, on the fucking BBC, because I'd have looked like a total cunt.

So I – I just riffed it, on the spot, I just riffed it.

Fuck knows why. I guess I –

And yeah, of course I felt *ashamed* – and the next morning I woke up with like a massive hangover – so I drank a bottle of whisky just so I could fucking sleep – and you know sometimes you wake up with this enormous fucking hungover *paranoia*, and you're like 'what the fuck did I do last night?' and then it dawns on you, with suddenly nightmarish clarity –

'Oh yeah, I lied about rescuing people out of a catastrophic plane crash on national TV.'

Not happened to you, right?

And you fucking brick yourself, mate. You fucking *brick* yourself.

And then I go out to get some Diet Coke to scare off the hangover, and I suddenly catch sight of all the newspapers on the newsagent's counter –

And my face is literally on the front of all of them.

And I'm like fuck fuck *fuck*.

And I buy some of the papers – basically so they'll be less of them, so I can, you know, hide my fucking embarrassment or something – and they're all about quoting my speech, and – beep, beep, beep – my phone starts going off, and it's going all morning, and all my mates and my mum and shit are phoning me, congratulating me, saying I'm a fucking hero, that I've given courage to the nation, all that shit.

And for the next couple of days I'm totally fucking terrified.

I feel like the sky is going to just collapse on my head. It twists my fucking guts.

I'm certain they're going to find me out, and when they do they're going to fucking *slaughter* me.

The newspapers, my mates, my mum, everybody, is going to fucking *slaughter* me.

My life is just this constant torture.

But they don't. Find out.

Nothing happens.

And my name has got out – probably one of my mates bragging in a pub – because I start getting these phone calls from the TV stations and stuff.

And for a week I say no, but they keep calling. All day the phone's ringing. Taunting the fuck out of me.

And you know what?

Nobody gets to be a hero, normally, do they? Not ever in your life.

I don't want to be one – but it's like everybody else kind of *wants* me to be one.

And eventually I kind of come to the conclusion that I'd be letting people down if I don't step up and be the person that everybody *needs* me to be.

The figurehead. The hero.

And over the next weeks and months, the fear just gradually recedes, and you start to *become* the thing you're pretending to be.

Fake it until you make it – you know, like in Alcoholics Anonymous.

And there's not a moment where I'm not ashamed of lying – but I reckon I've atoned for it – I reckon that I've caused far more good than bad.

I've given people hope, and courage, and, you know – all that.

Nobody's *really* a hero. Not really. Everybody has feet of clay, don't they?

But right now I've got a fucking problem, haven't I?

I'm sitting in the pub with this posh cunt, and he's found me out.

And I swear to God, I think about killing him, just to keep everything quiet.

And I'm sitting in the pub, thinking about how I'm going to do it – follow him home and strangle him – whatever –

And he just says –

(*Absurd posh voice*.) 'Seventy-thirty in my favour.'

And I'm like – 'What you chatting about, mate?'

And he's like,

ALEX. You've just got yourself an agent, *mate*, and my rates are seventy per cent of your gross earnings from the book for the next two years. Or I fuck. You. Up.

GRAHAM. And I'm like – 'Sixty-forty.'

And he looks at me, and he just smiles.

Scene Five

A different feel on the stage. Time has passed.

They're all on stage.

ANA. So the one-year anniversary of the BU21 crash was –

The memorial service I didn't attend.

People *remembering* the crash is really not the problem. It's people trying to *forget* the crash that's the problem, you know, you fuckers?

I watched it on television, though. I sort of *had* to. God knows why. The politicians did their preposterous speeches, and Graham, who wrote that book, did a speech as well.

That was quite good, actually.

At least he, you know, understands what it was like to be there.

In the group this week – I'm going again, by the way – Derek asked us all, 'What did you learn about yourself over the past year?'

And some people said inner strength and determination, all that stuff, but for me, I realised one thing.

When I was in the park that morning, screaming in agony, I wanted to die. Begged for it. But life was too strong.

And that afternoon a few months back, in my kitchen, I wanted to die also. But again, life was too strong.

Because, you know, life will fight for itself, tooth and claw, however hopeless the situation – because it's an animal, you know – *compulsion* –

It's almost completely impossible to resist, the ancient biological urge to live.

Often I wish I could.

Anyway – I'm doing good. Well, better. I'm working three mornings a week at a charity – at the BU21 Survivors' Group, actually.

Just at reception, you know? But it's something. It's a start.

And I guess one day I will feel hope again, but for now, I live because I *have* to.

Thank you for listening.

ANA *leaves*.

ALEX. So I guess this is the sort of wrap-up bit, the 'moral' of the fucking story. Never been massively up on morals, so –

Look – one day your life's probably going to fall to shit, like mine has. I mean, your girlfriend probably won't be burnt to death by a falling plane while being fucked from behind by your best mate, that's statistically pretty fucking rare –

But one day things are going to turn to shit for you, for one reason or another. And how are you going to cope with it?

Will you boss it like a boss? Or are you going to cave in like a fucktard?

That's the question to pose yourself, yeah? And if the answer's 'cave in' – do something about it, yeah? Change.

So I moved to a hedge fund in Mayfair – onwards and fucking upwards, you know –

And it was at the Christmas party, I reckon, where I had this – this stunning moment of transcendent insight about myself.

Well, I say Christmas party, but actually it was just me and six Lithuanian prostitutes in a hotel room at the Lanesborough.

That's a *proper* party, yeah?

I'd bought enough charlie to precisely recreate the snow scenes you see on the Christmas cards – I actually could have covered a charming old Cotswolds hamlet in pure-driven cocaine, you know?

But I didn't, obviously, I put it all in my nose in the prescribed manner.

I can just picture all those carol singers, you know – with their fucking lanterns – standing ankle-deep in my Christmas blow, all singing much more loudly and stridently than usual – all Santa's fucking reindeer with their noses jammed to the ground – Rudolf's taken so much that his nose goes red and his reindeer septum falls out his nose – all that shit.

And I looked at the prostitutes, and suddenly things became really *thrillingly* clear to me.

It's the professional lack of intimacy – doing their job, fucking well, utterly without emotional commitment.

Professionalism, man. It's the most beautiful thing in the world.

And it's something I've kind of built into my own life, you know? The best way to really, truly flourish in this world is to keep this minimal *distance*. It's like the *opposite* of mindfulness – I call it *mindlessness*. Never be – (*Ridiculous Californian voice.*) *present.*

(*Normal voice.*) Always be *absent*.

Avoiding pain while maximising pleasure. The maths of a good life. Not letting anything close enough to fucking hurt you.

Fucking works.

So the money I got from that Graham cunt, you know what I blew that on?

Yeah, bet you can't guess.

Maybe you can.

Yeah, predictably I spunked that all the to BU21 Survivors' Charity.

Six hundred and twenty-eight grand.

Come on, what did you think I'd do with it? I'm not a *total* cunt.

And it's fucking tax efficient, donating to charity.

See you fucking later. I'll be in the bar after if you're hot and available. No strings.

Although, looking around tonight – pretty ropey so – (*Finds somebody in the audience.*)

Fuck it, any port in a storm. If you can't be with the one you love, love the one you're with.

Seeya in a sec.

ALEX *leaves*.

CLIVE. Love is – it's changed me utterly.

Because I've realised that heaven isn't a place in the sky where you go when you die, it's here and now.

Head. Literally. Blown.

Floss is like – all the purity and truth and passion and clarity and love I used to think, at one point in my life, you could only get from God, from the divine – you get much more of that shit in *one afternoon* up in Floss's room than in an *eternity* in heaven.

Especially if you've got just a tiny little bit of MDMA.

The really weird thing is, right – love is – basically your soul experiences it as this huge *catastrophe* – I can't sleep, can't concentrate, I get randomly weepy at inappropriate points, my head's just all over the place, you know? And the *enormously* odd thing is that that's exactly how I felt when my dad died – the symptoms are *exactly the same* – only this time they're good symptoms, not bad symptoms.

That's so fucked up, isn't it?

It's kinda like human beings are these weirdly badly constructed mechanisms, like they were built by these really dodgy workmen who botched all the emotional... cabling. Got it all patched into the wrong places.

Sorry, that doesn't even make sense.

This year I've been the saddest I've ever been, and now I'm the happiest.

And I never could have predicted – and that's the thing about life – the most important, magical thing about life, I think – you can never, ever predict stuff. Sometimes unexpected shit happens that fucks your shit up, really, really badly – but also, it goes the other way – even if you're really, really sad and fucked up today – tomorrow, you might find yourself totally, unpredictably, happy –

You just never know. And that's the most beautiful thing in the world.

Love, man. It's all about love. That's all you need to know.

CLIVE *leaves*.

THALISSA. It's not like I'm one of those girls that like *defines* themselves by whether they're married.

But it's fucking nice, you know, now it's about to happen.

Alex is – he's a *guy*, he's a bit – a bit uncommunicative about things sometimes, a bit *surly*, a bit snarling and supercilious – a bit like he hates me, sometimes, like when he talks to me every word just drips this *contempt*, sometimes – but in his own way, I think he's as happy as me. About us.

And it's not that I want to *change* him – I'm not one of those mean ball-busty girls – but I think I can help him to be more – to develop and flourish and bloom. As a person.

The wedding's going to be *stunning*.

Look – I'm definitely not all bridezilla about it, you know – it's not like it fills *all* of my time, thinking about it, planning it – just *most of it*.

I'm totally joking.

I'm very – my sister's in events management – so we can totally smash this biatch.

Of course Mum's not going to be there – which is – almost unbearable, at times – but I think she'll look down from whenever she is, and she'll be totally overjoyed.

All she ever wanted was for her daughters to be happy, to be settled. So I've sort of got a duty to be happy, for her sake. To make her proud of us.

And I've changed, but I think I've also grown.

I guess that I embrace life more than ever now, because I know how precious it is, how fragile it is.

It's weird, isn't it, I've become *stronger* because I realise how *fragile* things are?

It's sort of beautiful, though, I think.

Wish me luck.

THALISSA *leaves*.

FLOSS. So in a couple of months I go back to university.

Do the second year, after like a year off.

I kind of think of it as a gap year – a grindingly, unremittingly horrific gap year. They kind of all are, though, aren't they? Actually it's been vastly more, you know, valuable than a *real* gap year – where you're in theory supposed to learn about yourself, and the world, and grow as a person – whereas in reality you just get boshed on shit speed and get off with a *heinous* rat-faced guy from Manchester called Gary in a sweaty tent somewhere in the third world – and to be frank, what the fuck does that teach you?

Whereas me? I learnt a bunch of shit.

And it's not good shit.

But it's the truth.

It's weird, all the houses are just being rebuilt so quickly. Everything's just getting back to normal –

The park's been relaid, the roads are working again, the shops, the offices –

I mean it always was a perpetual building site around here –

So if you *didn't* know, you totally *wouldn't* know.

But *we* know. *We* can't forget.

Once you've seen the truth you can't unsee it.

Ana the Roasted Romanian at the support group. That's what I'm talking about.

She was doing so well – we all thought she was doing so well.

But in the end she still killed herself. Last month. Yeah, I know. Which is fucking hard for all of us.

It turns out the only thing you really learn is that there's a certain magnitude of horror that you just can't deal with – that we're not programmed to deal with, as humans –

And when your glass is full, that's it – whatever you do, however heroically you fight it, it still fucking breaks you.

Cheery, yeah?

So I ended it with Clive a while back. My head was just – the fact that his dad randomly died in my back garden wasn't ever going to be the basis for a lasting relationship, was it?

I mean, it was fucking difficult to explain at parties, and –
between you and me – his coming face was fucking similar
to his dad's dying face –

Look, sorry, that was unforgiveable of me. I fucking realise,
okay? I'm just – I'm just – if you can't laugh at it it'll
fucking rip you to bits, yeah? And I'm not going to let that
happen, K?

We're still friends. Kinda. He took it a bit – he's grown a
beard. Goes to mosque a bunch of times a day now,
according to his Facebook.

Look, I'm sorry, but what the fuck did you expect?

(*Suddenly very emotional.*) Did you expect this to be a bunch
of happy fucking endings?

What the fuck?

You don't get better from this shit, okay?

Right, is that it?

Is this over now?

Why isn't this over now?

GRAHAM. Look, love, let me just – I need to do my bit, okay,
and then we can all finish? You just stay there, and I'll –
everybody's had their turn, you know?

(*To us.*) Right.

Epilogue

GRAHAM, *addressing a public event*.

GRAHAM (*making a speech*). Your Majesty, Prime Minister, ladies and gentlemen –

On the 22nd of July last year the lives of the people of Fulham – and indeed lives across London, the United Kingdom, and around the world – changed utterly.

BU21, flying from New York to London, crashed at thirty-two minutes past ten after being hit by an anti-aircraft missile. Five hundred and thirty-eight people died, and over two thousand were injured.

These are the bare facts of what happened, but underneath these facts – horrific and barbaric as they are – are many thousands of stories.

There are stories of loss, of grief, and of heartbreak.

But there are also stories of heroism, of astonishing kindness, and of communities pulling together.

And I say to you now, ladies and gentlemen, that our stories of hope proclaim far louder than our stories of despair.

My own story is well known, but I say this to you now – I am nothing.

Truly I am nothing, ladies and gentlemen, compared to the great spirit of the British people – a spirit which will overcome any obstacle, and any foe, today, and tomorrow, and for ever.

Today is not a day for politics. Today is a day of commemoration. And commemorate we must.

But every one of us has a sacred duty to remember that our great nation has come through times of great darkness and tribulation before, and we have emerged victorious.

And victorious we will emerge again.

Thank you.

(*In his normal voice*). I said all that, you know, at the service of commemoration.

And they cheered. Fuck me did they cheer.

And I looked up at myself on the giant screens, this one man alone in front of thousands and thousands of people, and I thought –

Boy done fucking good. Boy done great.

The End.

A Nick Hern Book

BU21 first published in Great Britain in 2016 as a paperback original by Nick Hern Books Limited, The Glasshouse, 49a Goldhawk Road, London W12 8QP, in association with Theatre503 and Kuleshov

Cover image: Lucy Newman

Designed and typeset by Nick Hern Books, London
Printed in Great Britain by Mimeo Ltd, Cambridgeshire PE29 6XX

A CIP catalogue record for this book is available from the British Library

ISBN 978 1 84842 573 6